# Calligraphy
# The Art of Beautiful Writing
## by
# Katherine Jeffares

A Tirzala Powers Publication

---

Published by

Melvin Powers
Wilshire Book Company
12015 Sherman Road
No. Hollywood, California 91605
telephone: (213) 875-1711

Printed in the United States of America

Library of Congress Catalog Card No.: 78-52137

ISBN: 0-87980-356-8

# Table of Contents

# Calligraphy III - Old English and Blackletter

## Slant Guides

Please note : The Platignum Nibs are slightly larger than the Osmiroid - therefore each slant guide has 2 nibs listed - the Osmiroid Nib size, then the Platignum.

# Calligraphy I

## The Traditional Art of Beautiful Writing

### The Chancery Cursive Hand

abcdefghijklm
nopqrstuvw
xyz

ABCDEFGHI
JKLMNOPQ
RSTUVW
XYZ

In Gratitude—

A special thanks goes to Adam Christensen for designing the original format based on Ludovico degli Arrighi's idea of learning each hand by families.

Also a special recognition to David Goines for certain letter forms, such as the special "r".

Finally another thanks to John Roger for inspiring me to return to the beautiful expression of calligraphy.

Kathy Jeffares

# Materials

## for beginning calligraphy

Fountain-Pen Sets:

There are two very good brands on the market: The Platignum and the Osmiroid. Both pens come in a Lettering Set with six nib inserts ranging in size from fine to the B4 which is the pen nib size I used to write the Chancery Cursive and Old English Alphabets. I prefer the Osmiroid 75 Lettering Set. If you are left-handed, be sure you buy a set marked left-handed.

Paper:

If you plan to use the lined guides in the back of the text book then purchase plain white paper (about 300 sheets) with 3 holes for a binder. Other college-ruled 3-hole binder paper can also be used if you use the unlined guide sheet.

Binder:

Please keep your practice sheets, samples and additional notes collected in a binder. Make sure it has large rings. That way you can organize your study of calligraphy.

Rag:

Keep a wash rag or paper towel handy to wipe your pen nib while in class. The writing edge of the pen nib should be kept clean and sharp for writing each letter. You may also wish to use the rag as a blotter when necessary.

Ink:

I suggest Pelikan Fount India Ink. It is one of the richest, blackest inks made and also very smooth. It will keep the pen nib flowing beautifully and also make writing easier. Osmiroid Free Flow inks, which

# Materials Continued

(Inks cont.) come also in other colors, are another excellent ink.

Optional Pen:
    A speedball pen holder with a C2 Broad Italic Nib is optional for those who wish to learn how to use the dip pen.    If you are left-handed be sure to purchase the pen marked left hand.

Books
    Besides this text you may want to purchase other calligraphic texts.    One of my favorites is:
Goines, An Introduction to the Elements of Calligraphy, Saint Heironymous Press, 1975.
Another good text is: Svaren, Written Letters: 22 Alphabets for Calligraphers, The Bond Wheelwright Company, 1975.

Miscellaneous Items:
    Pouch for your binder that holds pens, pencils, erasers, ruler, etc.
    Or a shoebox, an old purse, or a fishing tackle box again to hold equipment.

. . . . . . . . . .

Please note:    The Chancery Cursive Alphabet
        and the Old English Alphabet are written
        with the Osmiroid B4 Pen.

# Please Note !!

# Exercises for warm-up in use of B4 pen nib

1ˢᵗ Exercise: hold the pen at a 45° angle so that the nib faces the left corner of the paper; then make zig-zags. When you write the Chancery Cursive, the pen nib must constantly face the upper left corner of the paper you are writing on.

2ⁿᵈ Exercise: hold the pen at a 45° angle and write across the page in squiggles. Remember to always keep this angle when writing the Chancery Cursive.

3ʳᵈ Exercise: hold pen at 45° angle, put the paper you are writing on in front of the slant guide on page and carefully draw these lines.

$\mathcal{T}$his is our "i"- shaped family of letters. Each letter begins with a sharp slanting stroke up and a clear simple down-stroke to form the various designs. The upstroke is the thinnest possible line your pen can create because it is on the 45° angle. This is called a tic. Next the stem is made on the slant guide and the letter ends with an upstroke, which in the case of the "i", "n", "m" and "u" is also on the 45° angle and is called a flic. (Use the slant guide on page 65 while writing).

i        i      i    ii   iiiii
         tic
         stem
         flic

j        j     j j     jury

n        n    in    in    inn

m        m    inm    mini    jim

u        u    vu    minimum

v        v    iv    vim

w        w    vw    win    wini

y        y    vy    yummy    y

r        r    ir    run    ruin

7

This is our second family of letters. The "a" part of each letter is made in one continuous stroke, without lifting the pen from the paper, at any time. Follow the arrows for ideal forming of each letter and practice them in rows to get the feeling for spacing, rhythm and design.    Then write the words listed.

a  a c o a    a man

d  c o d    dad dandy

g  c o g    gag again

q  c o q    quince quid

d  d d dad    dad day d

These two "d's" are optional. They are made with one stroke.

8

This group of letters is also based on the "a" shape although they are often thought of as an "o" family. They are presented here as a continuation of the "a" family because in the Chancery Cursive Alphabet, these letters are formed with the same movement of the pen as the "a".

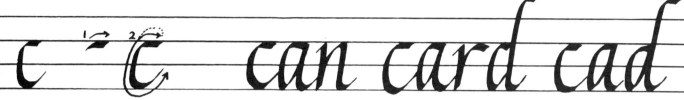

c c can card cad

The bottom part of the "c" should extend further than the top in order to provide a clear joining to the next letter.

e e eden eddy

The bottom part of the "e" should also extend further than the top for the same reason.

o o one odor

The "o" is drawn similarly to the "a" except that it is given a rounder curve as it is completed.

Practice the above letters in rows at first: ccccc eeeee ooooo. Then begin to form word combinations. Be aware when writing words of the slant of each letter.

Try these words: coin, energy, dove, groove, quince, oven, deer, dear, cave, move, noon, moon june, ear, corn or corn, can, good, queen, gear, young.
See page for words to trace.

Our next group of letters is based on the "l" shape. As you can see the long stroke forms the axis of the letters with the "f" being the longest miniscule in this alphabet. Long stemmed letters that reach above the middle line are called "ascenders"; letters moving below the middle line are called "descenders."

l l ll  all holly

h h h  honey  hall

k l l k  kiwi knuckle

b b b  blue bell

f f f  for fluffy

r gr or wring  krk

This form of the "r" is used only when there is a smooth-bodied letter preceding it, to give the support and suggestion of a stem.

And these are our miscellaneous letters which partake of characteristics of our other families but truly are unique to themselves.

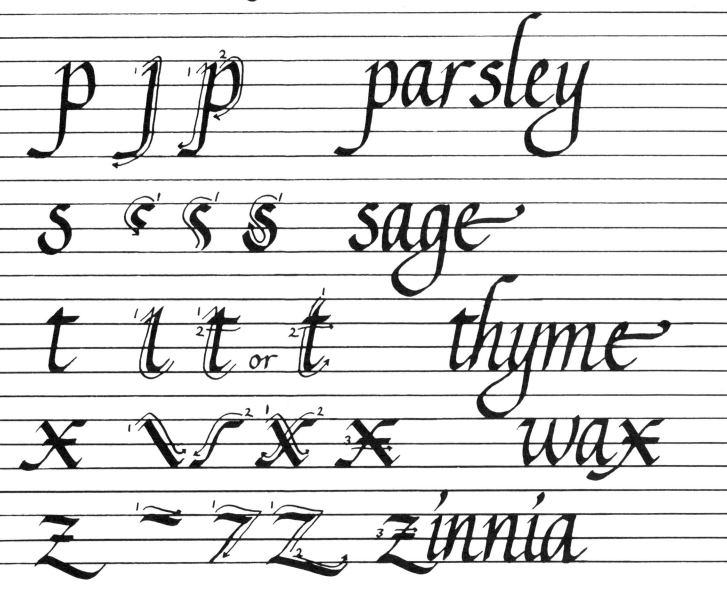

p    p j p    parsley

s    s s s s s    sage

t    t t t t t or t    thyme

x    x v x x x    wax

z    z z z z z    zinnia

Now you have learned all of the minuscules of the Chancery Cursive Alphabet. Play with them; it is truly a delight to take up your pen and let your imagination flow while watching beautiful letters appear on your paper!!

# Capitals

in the Chancery Cursive Hand

A l M Alice A Andy

B l b Bill Bob

C C C Cathy Charles

D l l David Daisy

E T L Ed Eve E

F T J Francis F for

G ℭ ℭ G George Gay G

H I I H Helen H Hank

I I I I Ida Ivan Irene

J J JJ Jacob Jeffrey

K I I K Kathy Ken

L I I L Lucille Lee

M I I N N Mandy M

13

N 'N 'N 'N Nadine 'Ned

O 'O 'O or 'O Odine

P J J Paul P Penelope

Q 'O 'O or O Quince

R R R Rodney R Rand

S Shirley S Sally

T T T Ted Taras To:

14

$\mathcal{U}$ $\mathcal{U}$ $\mathcal{V}$ Ursula $\mathcal{U}$

$\mathcal{V}$ $\mathcal{V}$ $\mathcal{V}$ Victor

$\mathcal{W}$ $\mathcal{V}$ $\mathcal{VU}$ Wendy $\mathcal{W}$

$\mathcal{X}$ $\mathcal{X}$ $\mathcal{X}$ Xray

$\mathcal{Y}$ $\mathcal{V}$ $\mathcal{V}$ Ynez Yvonne

$\mathcal{Z}$ $\mathcal{Z}$ $\mathcal{Z}$ Zee

Now you've learned the entire alphabet. The key to success is practice plus enjoyment: a generous helping of both will turn your letters into a beautiful art.

# Numbers & Punctuation

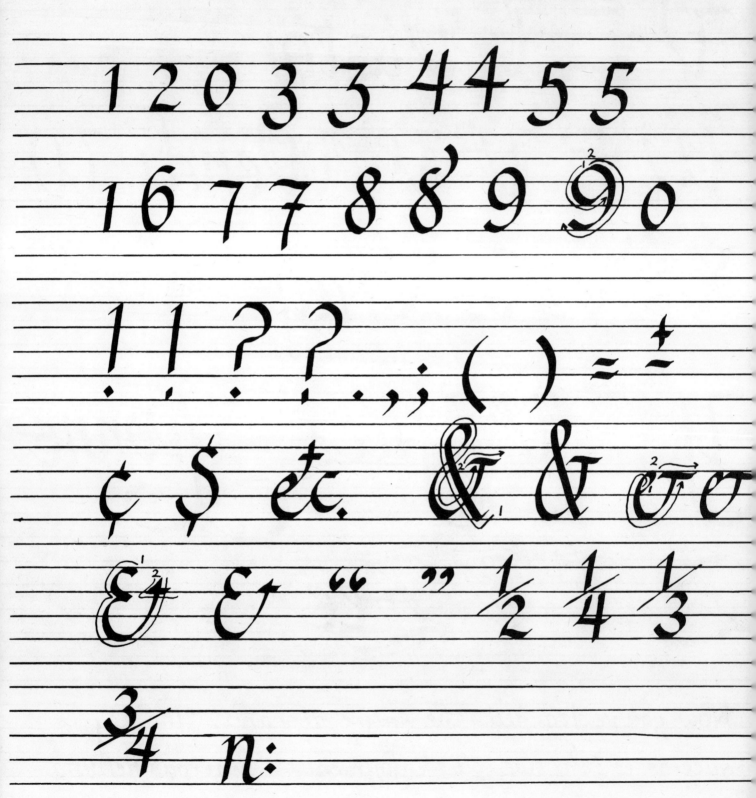

1 2 0 3 3 4 4 5 5

1 6 7 7 8 8 9 9 0

1 1 ? ? . , ; ( ) = ÷

ç $ etc. & & ctʒ

& & " " ½ ¼ ⅓

¾ n:

coin energy grow

groove dove quince

oven deer cave me

dear moon june ear

corn can good gear

candy queen que

many young

# Letters for tracing

a e i o u c

b h k fx d d k

g j y l ll p q

m n r s t u v q

w w y x z

# More Letters For Tracing

A A A A A B B
C C C D D E E
E F F F F G
G G H H H I
I In Joe Jim K
K K K L L L M

19

# More Letters For Tracing

M N N O Q P Pa

P P R R R S S

S J T T T Jo

U V V W X X

Y Y Z

# Pen Nib Widths

5　a e i o u m n v

5　c r s w w x z

10　l h b k k d B D

10　p y g j g　For To

8　t t A E　and all Capitals

the size of the A or E

15　f　12　L Paul

# Pen Nib Widths & Slant Guides

The slant guides are listed in the back of the textbook and each one shows in the right hand corner the correct pen nib for each guide. The Osmiroid Nib size is listed first, then the Platignum size. You may wish to make your own guide for the fine nib by doubling the lines of the B2 guides.

# Formula for Cleaning Pen Nibs

In a quart jar of water put 1 tablespoon of ammonia and 1 tablespoon of any liquid detergent. Seal jar with a cap until ready to use. Then shake contents and pour one inch of liquid into a plastic cup. Place pen nib into solution. Let sit overnight. Pour out contents and rinse off nib with plain water.

# Calligraphy II
## Illumination
## &
## Adam's Bookhand
## Alphabet

# Materials for Illumination

To illuminate a piece of calligraphy means to brighten and decorate it with beautiful designs, especially foliage, birds, butterflies, and whatever else comes to mind. Examine the works of other calligraphers and illuminators through out the Middle Ages and later periods of art to learn their techniques and styles. Then adventure forth in your own original expression.

The tools we'll need are:

1. A set of watercolors: either P.H. Martins Radiant Concentrated Watercolors or Luma Concentrated Watercolors: six colors to start with: Alpine Rose or a red hue, Violet, Moss Green, True Blue, Lemon Yellow, and Coffee Brown.

2. Small sable brushes #1~3 in size.

3. Platignum or Osmiroid Pen Set. The Platignum Lettering Set contains a wider range of nibs than the Italic Set.

4. Kneaded Eraser.

5. A 12" or 18" ruler or right angle. The plastic "see thru" ruler is probably best.

6. A book of poetry or famous quotations for inspiration on what to write.

7. A set of marker pens with a fine point. A set of 8 is sufficient. Pentel is an excellent brand.

8. The black pilot pen for fine line drawings.

9. Canson tracing pad with sketching scale, size 9"x 12".
or

10. Aquabee, white Calligraphy pad; size 9"x 12"; also comes in antique color.

11. Plain 3 hole typing paper and a binder to hold the paper for practice sheets.

12. The design-art pen with a chisel point #492. A set of six basic colors would be good for a starter. This last item is optional.

13. You may also want to purchase Pelikan Fount India Ink to replace Pelikan 4001 ink.

Stippling is a technique used throughout the Middle Ages to beautify the introductory majuscule of a written piece. It is simply outlining the letter in dots. This gives it a depth and shimmering quality and, though simply done, makes the letter special and interesting.

This "B" was drawn with the "E4" steel brush and the stippling done with a Platignum italic penpoint, fine nib size. The most beautiful results of this technique are created by colored inks or marker pens, the bold body of the capital drawn in one color and light misting of the stipple drawn in a complementary color. Complementary colors are opposite each other on the color wheel. They are red-green, orange-blue and yellow-purple.

In order to do this technique you need a fine nib point and different colored inks, dyes or marker pens.

26

A B C D E
F G H I J
K L M N
O P Q R S
T U V W etc...

27

Flourishes are grace strokes added to the tradition-al design of a letter. The variety of flourishes is infinite but study and practice the following examples in order to develop your own style. As long as the letter is legible and the flourish is pleasing, be as creative as you like.

Often in designing someone's name, the pattern of the letters suggests a way of flourishing so that the name is joined together or encircled by a beautiful pattern. One of the main uses of the flourish is to create beautiful names, monograms or plaques.

Mary Springfield

Ligatures are artistic lines drawn to connect certain letters to each other. They are used in calligraphy to enliven the written line.

Letter combinations like ct, cp, ck, st, sp and sk use the overhead ligature.

sky star sparrow

arcturus ck cp ct

celestial spheres

filigree fi first

The fi ligature is often seen in print. In calligraphy it is also very naturally drawn.

Joining the T and h is also a very popular written device.

The Thespian

*Ligatures (cont.)* To draw the basic ligature, simply write your two letters and tie them together ... this way:

st · cat · cab · cod · ch ·

cafe · clean · check ·

cap · court · cut · clams

snob · sad · soft · shake

skate · slack · spot

Notice in the "sp" ligature that the tie may have a deeper curve than the other. This is because the stem of the "p" is lower than the other letters which are ascending letters and, of course, have taller stems than the other letters. Most ligatures are used with ascending letters and the "c" and "s" letters.

Ligatures (cont.)

A little fancier version of the ligature is like this:

Star · drawn like this: ß · ß · ßt

This may also be used with the sk·sp·sh·sf·sl combinations.

sky · spirit · shine · sleep

This is true of the ck·cp·ch·cf·cl· combinations.

characters · childhood

Use this fanciest version sparingly; it is very lovely and looks best when it is used in an otherwise flourish-barren piece of writing, as a surprise to add life and interest.

"As the first glance from
the eyes of the beloved
is like a seed sown in
the human heart
And the first kiss of
her lips like a flower
upon the branch of
the Tree of Life....."

KAHLIL
GIBRAN

Examples of Ligatures

Illumination in writing is achieved very easily by enlarged initial letters which may be embedded in the page or drawn in the margin, or with the stem of the letter trailing down the margin for accent.

In the traditional style, the written lines proceed from the upper part of the enlarged initial rather than the bottom of the initial. The style of the initial may be the same as the written line but most often it will be distinctly different, either classical Roman, Versal, Blackletter or some other, even invented, letter. This method will add a bit of flair to the page.

To get acquainted with other alphabets, this text describes three other types that could be used. Also most libraries have good reference books on the design of letters.

Illumination (cont.) When working with color, remember that black is heavier than any color, and so you must adjust the weight of your initial so that it carries a stronger accent than the written lines. Also, be consistent in your use of other decorative items, such as, the use of flourishes and ligatures, using a few but not over-accent- ing the page.

Keep your margins clean and neat. It adds so much to the appeal of your art work. Use paper that comes in a tablet with graph sheets included or make your own graph sheets for each pen nib size you desire to use. This text provides you with slant guides for the Platignum B2, B3 and B4.

# As a man thinketh in his heart so he becomes.

The doubled "A" in this inscription of a proverb sets off the text and brings it more to life. Using colored inks or marker pens for the doubling can also be a wonderful way of decorating your writing.

A B C D E F
G H I J J K
L M N
O P R Q S S
T U V W
X Y Z

## Double-Lettering

One of the best way
to use this techniqu
is with two ink
colors ~ one color for
the main body and
the other for the doubl

36

A B C D E

F G H I J

K L M N

O P Q R S

T U V W

ℓc.

*Simple Shadow Lettering*

37

# Shadow Lettering
## for a card

# Happy
# Birthday

# Bookhand Alphabet

abcdefghijklm
nopqrstuvw
xyz

ABCDEFG
HIIJKLM
NNOPQRS
TUVWX
YZ

# Bookhand Alphabet

This alphabet was designed by Adam Christensen. It is made up essentially of round-bodied letters and straight stems. This style is best used with titles, announcements, and any lettering task where you need a hand-lettering that appears bold and noticeable.

When writing with this alphabet, think always of the appearance of your round-shaped letters, making them full and sweet like a very round apple. The more perfectly round you draw them, the better. This brings out the stability of the letters and makes for an even marriage in style between the o-shape and the s-shape or stem. It is a child-like alphabet, similar to the first alphabet we all learned when we were beginning to print in kindergarten or first grade.

The Chancery Cursive style is drawn on a definite slant, and if you master both these alphabets, you have a beautiful repertoire of style to create just about any kind of lettered creation you might like to do or be asked to do. They complement each other and you may want to use a Bookhand majuscule with an inscription drawn in chancery cursive; or vice-versa.

The small letters for the Bookhand Alphabet were written with the Osmiroid B 3 pen nib. Try tracing the letters first to get a feel for each letter, then write them on your own.

# The Bookhand Alphabet - minuscules

This is the first family of bookhand minuscules. It is made essentially from a round c-like stroke and a simple straight stroke with variations according to the different letters.

a c a²    a a a a a a

d c d²    d d d·dad

g c g²    g g gg·gad

q c q²    q q q q

c c c    c c c·cad

e e²    e e e·deed

o c o    o o o·go·goad

Be sure to make your round strokes very round and full and your straight strokes clearly straight with a diagonal beginning to make the stem of the letter shapely.    The serif or grace stroke on the tail of the "g" is optional.  The serif on the "e" is used at the end of a sentence or paragraph.

# The Second Family

The Second Family of bookhand letters emphasizes the long stem. Practice the "l" to become familiar with the making of the long stem.

l l l    log · load · lad · all

h l h    had · hall · head

k l k k    keg · kale · keel

b l b b    babe · bed

f f f    fad · food · fed

The tall stem letters begin with a flag type stroke (except the "f" which begins with a hook shape) and end with a cut-look. This cut-look is a part of many of the letters in this family and other small letters in this alphabet. The tip of the cut comes right to the bottom line. Sometimes a serif is added like a foot on to the "h" but "h" can be written without it.

i i i    idle · giggle · hill

j j j    jade · jag · jack

n i n n    in · need · inn

m i n m    mime · mimic

p i p    pin · pip · pipe

r i r    recline · refer

u u u    rough · hugh

W or w    won · winner

V or v    vim · veil · vary

y y y y    young · yon

# Notes on the Third Family

These letters make use of a beginning stem with the exception of the u and the w, which have their stems at the end of the letter, and the v which is included because of its closeness in style to the u, w and y; it is really a letter of its own.

The slight line at the beginning of these letters is the tic which is also used in the Chancery Cursive Alphabet. But in the writing of the u, w, and y, a serif is used in place of the tic.

The u is an upside down n; the w is an upside down m. Practice making the end stem - stroke of the u or w so that it ex-actly encloses the shape of the u or w.

Make sure all the stems are very straight and the round part of each letter is very round.

S S S     sun sassy

t t     three toys little

X X     x-ray xerox

z z     zebra zipper

The "s" is drawn very upright and full with a top smaller than the bottom, and both full and round.

The "t" is drawn with a beginning angle stroke and then a simple broadstroke ending a wee bit below the line like the "f". The "bar of the "t" is drawn just slightly above the smaller letters.

The "x" is drawn like the beginning of a "v", ending with a joining dash; the second stroke is lighter with small serifs at each end.

The "z" is drawn like a chancery cursive "z" without the long swing of the tail.

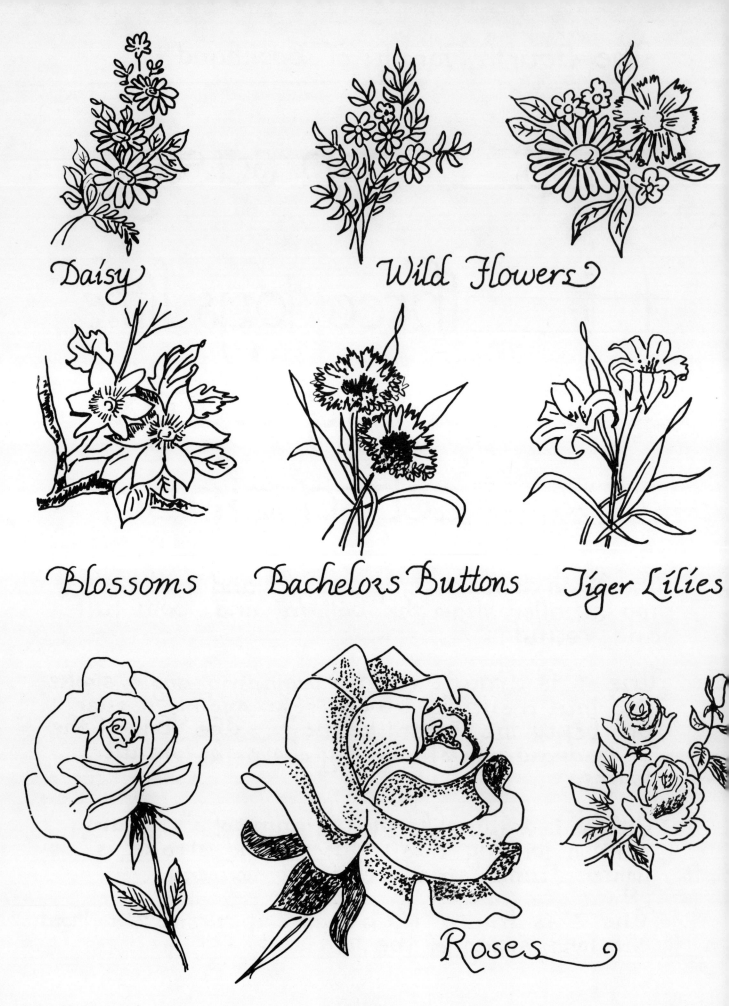

Daisy

Wild Flowers

Blossoms

Bachelors Buttons

Tiger Lilies

Roses

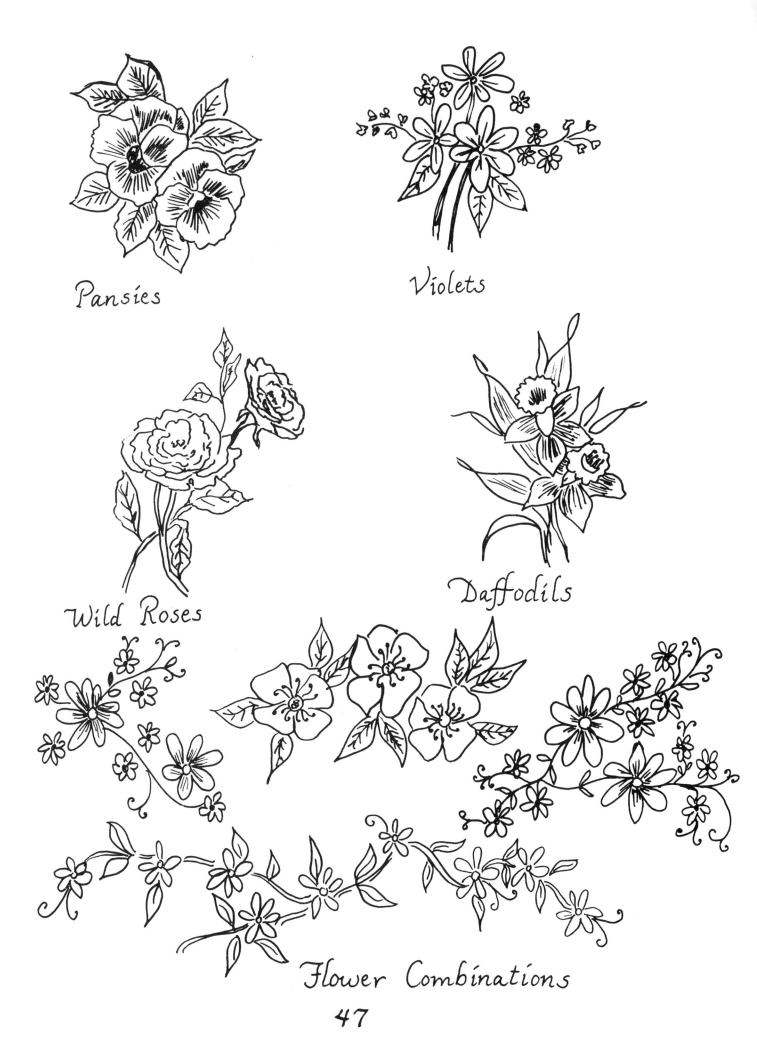

Pansies

Violets

Wild Roses

Daffodils

Flower Combinations

47

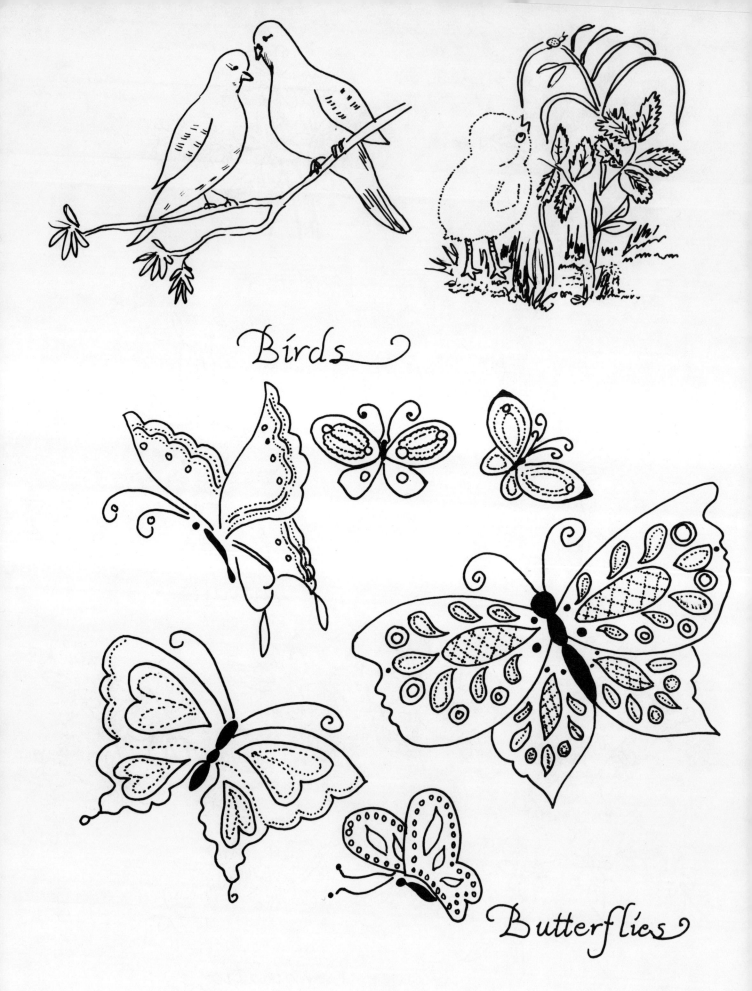

Birds

Butterflies

48

Borders

49

# Calligraphy II

# Old English & Blackletter

# Old English

ABCDEFGH
IJKLMNO
PQRSTUV
WXYZ

abcdefghijkl
mnopqrs tuv
wxyz

# the "i" family

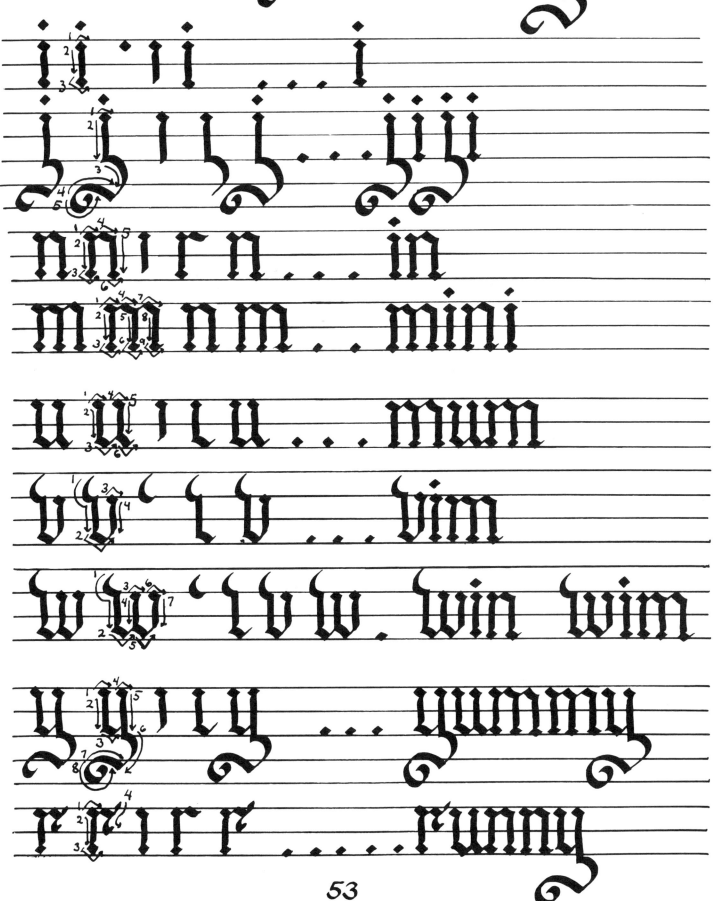

# the "o" Family

c c ˙ c c . . . civic

d d ˙ c c d . . . drum

e e ˙ c e . . . end den

g g ˙ c g g . energy

o o ˙ c o . . . order door

p p ˙ c p p . . pun

q q ˙ c q q . . quinine

# the "l" Family

ll·ll.....lily

hh·lhh....holly

kkl·k....lark

bbl·b...bee bell

ff·ff....flower

t·tft...thyme

# odd letters

a a a a .....oak after

s s ᷐ c s s ....sage

x x x x x ...flax

z z ᷮ ᷮ z z ...zinnia

*All of the minuscules of the "Old English"
were made with the osmiroid B4 point.*

# Capitals

A /\\ /\\ Alice

B 3 B B Bill

C C C C Cathy

D ) ) Don

E [ [ [ Edith

F [ [ [ Faith

G G G G Grace

h l l h Harry

J J J J Jvy

J J J J James

k l l l l kathy

l l l l Larry

M ſ ſ ſ M Mary

N \ \ \ Ned

O O O O Ophelia

P P P P Philip

Q O Q Q Quince

R l R R Robert

59

S S S S Sally

T T T Timothy

U I I I U Ursula

V V VV Vicky

W VVV William

# X X Xavior

# Y Y Y Youngman

# Z Z Zebra

Capitals were printed with the
B4 Osmiroid pen.

# Numbers

1 2 3 4 5 6 7

8 9 0

# Punctuation

. ? X , ; ¢ $

" " & ( )

# Blackletter

abcdefghijkl
mnopqrstuv
wxyz

# A B C D E F G
# H I J K M L N
# O P Q R S T
# U V W X Y Z

# Blackletter
# Capitals

7° Slant
for Chancery
Cursive

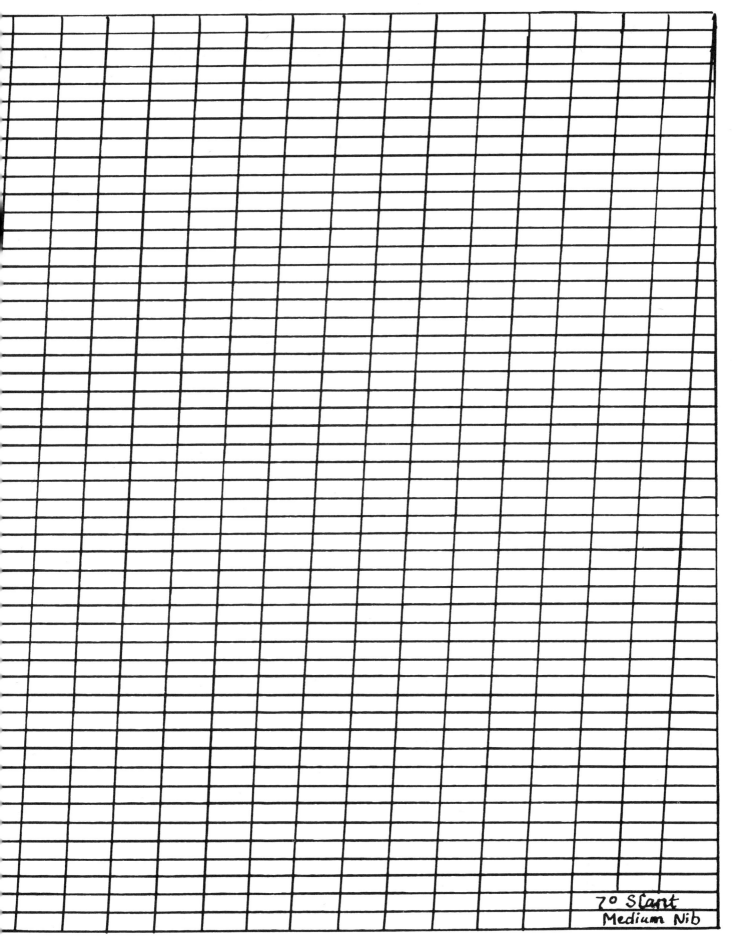

7° Slant
Medium Nib

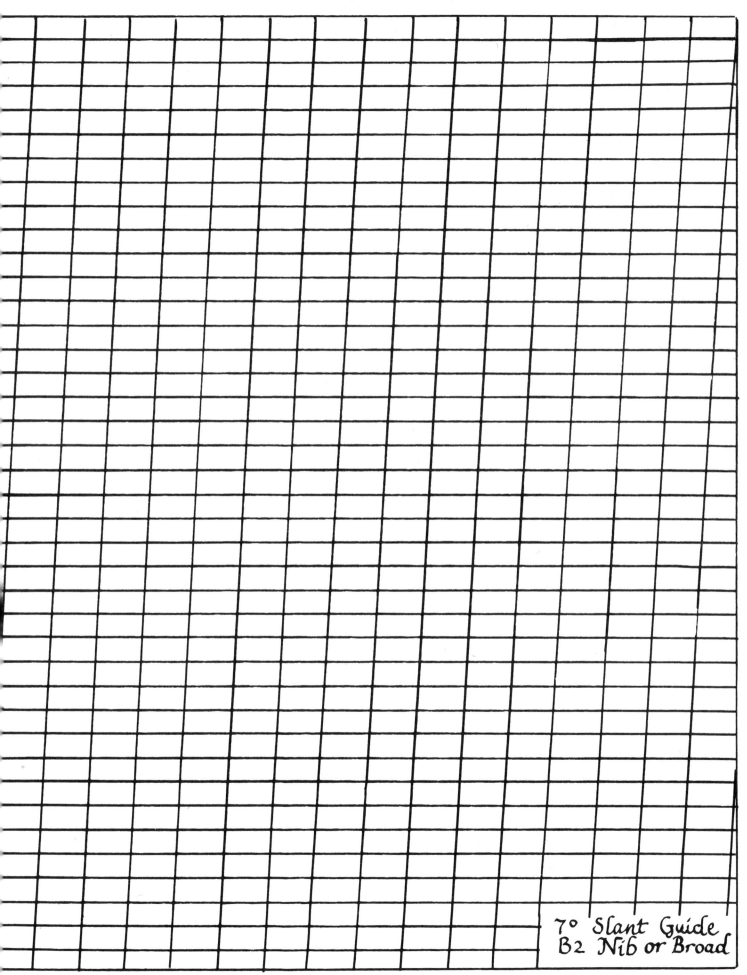

7° Slant Guide
B2 Nib or Broad

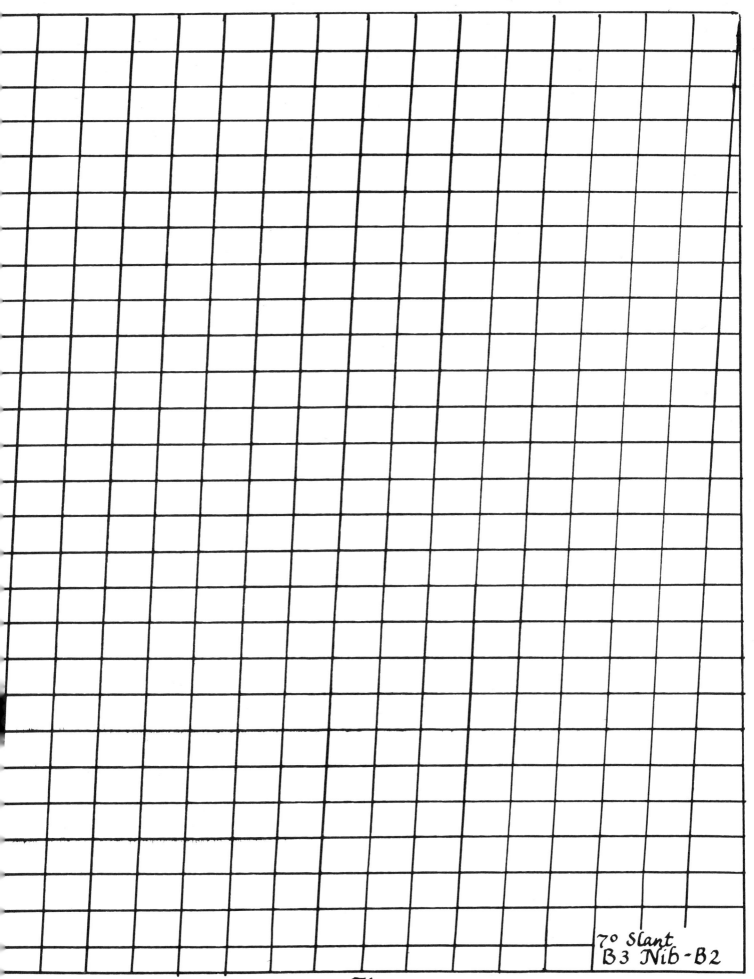

7° Slant
B3 Nib - B2

7° Slant
B4 Nib
B3 Nib

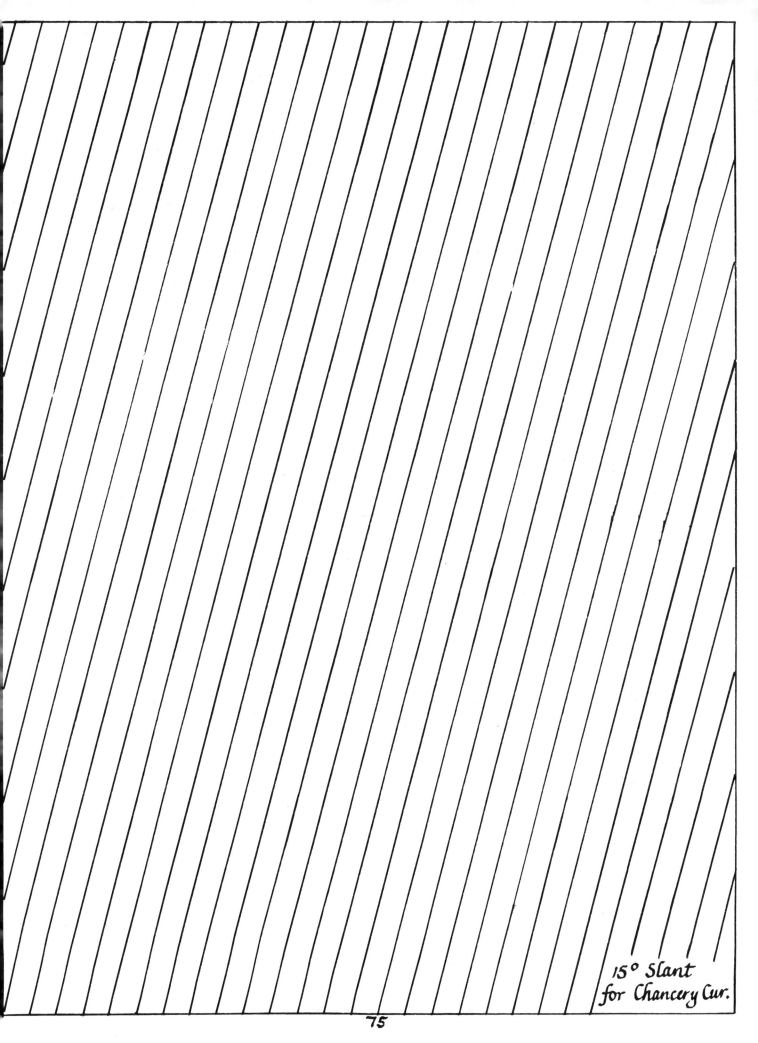

15° Slant
for Chancery Cur.

75

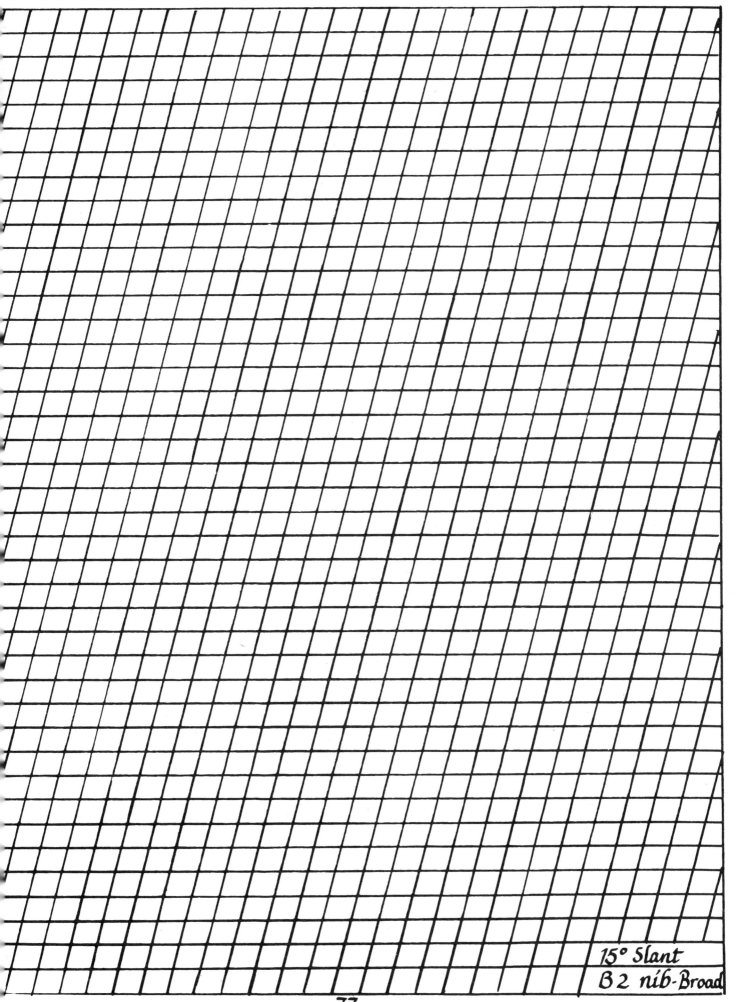

15° Slant
B 2 nib-Broad

77

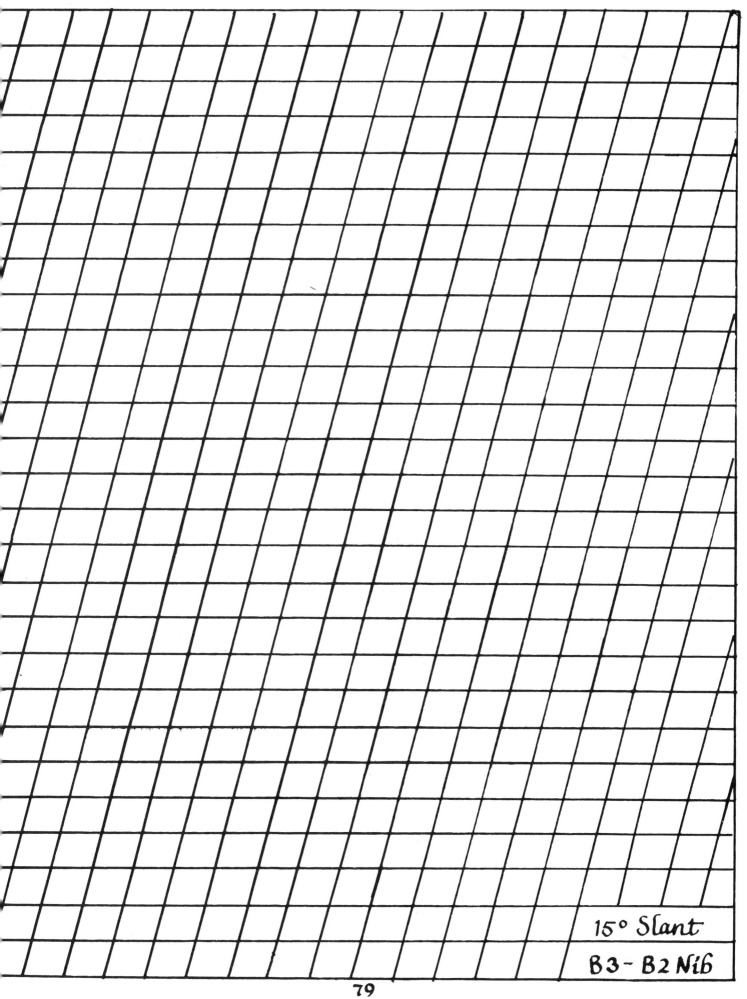

15° Slant

B3 - B2 Nib

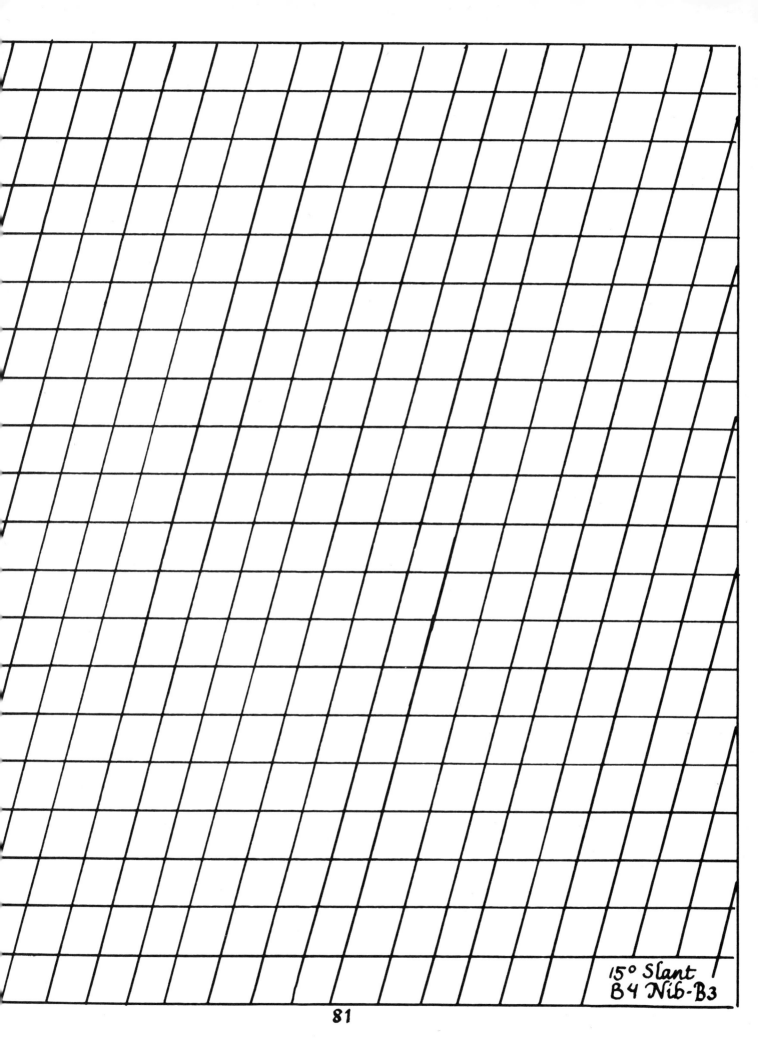

15° Slant
B4 Nib-B3

83

0° Slant Guide for
Bookhand & Old English

# A Personal Note From Kathy Jeffares

Dear Friend:

I hope you have enjoyed my basic book on Calligraphy and are now writing beautifully and finding pleasure in your newly found skill. Pride and satisfaction can be found in this artistic, communicative expression.

For your continued interest and to further enhance your calligraphic abilities, I suggest you obtain my new book, <u>Advanced Calligraphy</u>. You will find three more styles of writing, plus ideas on decorating and gold leafing and one chapter of the works of some of my students, which you could use as guides in creating your own works of art.

You can obtain this new book through your local bookstore or directly from my publisher. Send $7.00 plus $1.00 postage and handling for <u>Advanced Calligraphy</u> by Kathy Jeffares to:

Melvin Powers
12015 Sherman Road
North Hollywood, California 91605

# MELVIN POWERS SELF-IMPROVEMENT LIBRARY

## ASTROLOGY
_____ ASTROLOGY: HOW TO CHART YOUR HOROSCOPE *Max Heindel* 3.00
_____ ASTROLOGY: YOUR PERSONAL SUN-SIGN GUIDE *Beatrice Ryder* 3.00
_____ ASTROLOGY FOR EVERYDAY LIVING *Janet Harris* 2.00
_____ ASTROLOGY MADE EASY *Astarte* 3.00
_____ ASTROLOGY MADE PRACTICAL *Alexandra Kayhle* 3.00
_____ ASTROLOGY, ROMANCE, YOU AND THE STARS *Anthony Norvell* 4.00
_____ MY WORLD OF ASTROLOGY *Sydney Omarr* 5.00
_____ THOUGHT DIAL *Sydney Omarr* 4.00
_____ WHAT THE STARS REVEAL ABOUT THE MEN IN YOUR LIFE *Thelma White* 3.00

## BRIDGE
_____ BRIDGE BIDDING MADE EASY *Edwin B. Kantar* 5.00
_____ BRIDGE CONVENTIONS *Edwin B. Kantar* 5.00
_____ BRIDGE HUMOR *Edwin B. Kantar* 3.00
_____ COMPETITIVE BIDDING IN MODERN BRIDGE *Edgar Kaplan* 4.00
_____ DEFENSIVE BRIDGE PLAY COMPLETE *Edwin B. Kantar* 10.00
_____ HOW TO IMPROVE YOUR BRIDGE *Alfred Sheinwold* 3.00
_____ IMPROVING YOUR BIDDING SKILLS *Edwin B. Kantar* 4.00
_____ INTRODUCTION TO DEFENDER'S PLAY *Edwin B. Kantar* 3.00
_____ SHORT CUT TO WINNING BRIDGE *Alfred Sheinwold* 3.00
_____ TEST YOUR BRIDGE PLAY *Edwin B. Kantar* 3.00
_____ WINNING DECLARER PLAY *Dorothy Hayden Truscott* 4.00

## BUSINESS, STUDY & REFERENCE
_____ CONVERSATION MADE EASY *Elliot Russell* 2.00
_____ EXAM SECRET *Dennis B. Jackson* 3.00
_____ FIX-IT BOOK *Arthur Symons* 2.00
_____ HOW TO DEVELOP A BETTER SPEAKING VOICE *M. Hellier* 3.00
_____ HOW TO MAKE A FORTUNE IN REAL ESTATE *Albert Winnikoff* 4.00
_____ INCREASE YOUR LEARNING POWER *Geoffrey A. Dudley* 2.00
_____ MAGIC OF NUMBERS *Robert Tocquet* 2.00
_____ PRACTICAL GUIDE TO BETTER CONCENTRATION *Melvin Powers* 3.00
_____ PRACTICAL GUIDE TO PUBLIC SPEAKING *Maurice Forley* 3.00
_____ 7 DAYS TO FASTER READING *William S. Schaill* 3.00
_____ SONGWRITERS RHYMING DICTIONARY *Jane Shaw Whitfield* 5.00
_____ SPELLING MADE EASY *Lester D. Basch & Dr. Milton Finkelstein* 2.00
_____ STUDENT'S GUIDE TO BETTER GRADES *J. A. Rickard* 3.00
_____ TEST YOURSELF—Find Your Hidden Talent *Jack Shafer* 3.00
_____ YOUR WILL & WHAT TO DO ABOUT IT *Attorney Samuel G. Kling* 3.00

## CALLIGRAPHY
_____ ADVANCED CALLIGRAPHY *Katherine Jeffares* 7.00
_____ CALLIGRAPHER'S REFERENCE BOOK *Anne Leptich & Jacque Evans* 6.00
_____ CALLIGRAPHY—The Art of Beautiful Writing *Katherine Jeffares* 7.00
_____ CALLIGRAPHY FOR FUN & PROFIT *Anne Leptich & Jacque Evans* 6.00
_____ CALLIGRAPHY MADE EASY *Tina Serafini* 7.00

## CHESS & CHECKERS
_____ BEGINNER'S GUIDE TO WINNING CHESS *Fred Reinfeld* 3.00
_____ BETTER CHESS—How to Play *Fred Reinfeld* 2.00
_____ CHECKERS MADE EASY *Tom Wiswell* 2.00
_____ CHESS IN TEN EASY LESSONS *Larry Evans* 3.00
_____ CHESS MADE EASY *Milton L. Hanauer* 3.00
_____ CHESS MASTERY—A New Approach *Fred Reinfeld* 3.00
_____ CHESS PROBLEMS FOR BEGINNERS *edited by Fred Reinfeld* 2.00
_____ CHESS SECRETS REVEALED *Fred Reinfeld* 2.00
_____ CHESS STRATEGY—An Expert's Guide *Fred Reinfeld* 2.00
_____ CHESS TACTICS FOR BEGINNERS *edited by Fred Reinfeld* 3.00
_____ CHESS THEORY & PRACTICE *Morry & Mitchell* 2.00
_____ HOW TO WIN AT CHECKERS *Fred Reinfeld* 3.00
_____ 1001 BRILLIANT WAYS TO CHECKMATE *Fred Reinfeld* 3.00
_____ 1001 WINNING CHESS SACRIFICES & COMBINATIONS *Fred Reinfeld* 3.00
_____ SOVIET CHESS *Edited by R. G. Wade* 3.00

## COOKERY & HERBS
_____ CULPEPER'S HERBAL REMEDIES *Dr. Nicholas Culpeper* 3.00

_____FAST GOURMET COOKBOOK *Poppy Cannon*    2.50
_____GINSENG The Myth & The Truth *Joseph P. Hou*    3.00
_____HEALING POWER OF HERBS *May Bethel*    3.00
_____HEALING POWER OF NATURAL FOODS *May Bethel*    3.00
_____HERB HANDBOOK *Dawn MacLeod*    3.00
_____HERBS FOR COOKING AND HEALING *Dr. Donald Law*    2.00
_____HERBS FOR HEALTH—How to Grow & Use Them *Louise Evans Doole*    3.00
_____HOME GARDEN COOKBOOK—Delicious Natural Food Recipes *Ken Kraft*    3.00
_____MEDICAL HERBALIST *edited by Dr. J. R. Yemm*    3.00
_____NATURAL FOOD COOKBOOK *Dr. Harry C. Bond*    3.00
_____NATURE'S MEDICINES *Richard Lucas*    3.00
_____VEGETABLE GARDENING FOR BEGINNERS *Hugh Wiberg*    2.00
_____VEGETABLES FOR TODAY'S GARDENS *R. Milton Carleton*    2.00
_____VEGETARIAN COOKERY *Janet Walker*    3.00
_____VEGETARIAN COOKING MADE EASY & DELECTABLE *Veronica Vezza*    3.00
_____VEGETARIAN DELIGHTS—A Happy Cookbook for Health *K. R. Mehta*    2.00
_____VEGETARIAN GOURMET COOKBOOK *Joyce McKinnel*    3.00

## GAMBLING & POKER

_____ADVANCED POKER STRATEGY & WINNING PLAY *A. D. Livingston*    3.00
_____HOW NOT TO LOSE AT POKER *Jeffrey Lloyd Castle*    3.00
_____HOW TO WIN AT DICE GAMES *Skip Frey*    3.00
_____HOW TO WIN AT POKER *Terence Reese & Anthony T. Watkins*    3.00
_____SECRETS OF WINNING POKER *George S. Coffin*    3.00
_____WINNING AT CRAPS *Dr. Lloyd T. Commins*    3.00
_____WINNING AT GIN *Chester Wander & Cy Rice*    3.00
_____WINNING AT POKER—An Expert's Guide *John Archer*    3.00
_____WINNING AT 21—An Expert's Guide *John Archer*    3.00
_____WINNING POKER SYSTEMS *Norman Zadeh*    3.00

## HEALTH

_____BEE POLLEN *Lynda Lyngheim & Jack Scagnetti*    3.00
_____DR. LINDNER'S SPECIAL WEIGHT CONTROL METHOD *P. G. Lindner, M.D.*    1.50
_____HELP YOURSELF TO BETTER SIGHT *Margaret Darst Corbett*    3.00
_____HOW TO IMPROVE YOUR VISION *Dr. Robert A. Kraskin*    3.00
_____HOW YOU CAN STOP SMOKING PERMANENTLY *Ernest Caldwell*    3.00
_____MIND OVER PLATTER *Peter G. Lindner, M.D.*    3.00
_____NATURE'S WAY TO NUTRITION & VIBRANT HEALTH *Robert J. Scrutton*    3.00
_____NEW CARBOHYDRATE DIET COUNTER *Patti Lopez-Pereira*    1.50
_____PSYCHEDELIC ECSTASY *William Marshall & Gilbert W. Taylor*    2.00
_____QUICK & EASY EXERCISES FOR FACIAL BEAUTY *Judy Smith-deal*    2.00
_____QUICK & EASY EXERCISES FOR FIGURE BEAUTY *Judy Smith-deal*    2.00
_____REFLEXOLOGY *Dr. Maybelle Segal*    3.00
_____REFLEXOLOGY FOR GOOD HEALTH *Anna Kaye & Don C. Matchan*    3.00
_____YOU CAN LEARN TO RELAX *Dr. Samuel Gutwirth*    3.00
_____YOUR ALLERGY—What To Do About It *Allan Knight, M.D.*    3.00

## HOBBIES

_____BEACHCOMBING FOR BEGINNERS *Norman Hickin*    2.00
_____BLACKSTONE'S MODERN CARD TRICKS *Harry Blackstone*    3.00
_____BLACKSTONE'S SECRETS OF MAGIC *Harry Blackstone*    3.00
_____COIN COLLECTING FOR BEGINNERS *Burton Hobson & Fred Reinfeld*    3.00
_____ENTERTAINING WITH ESP *Tony 'Doc' Shiels*    2.00
_____400 FASCINATING MAGIC TRICKS YOU CAN DO *Howard Thurston*    3.00
_____HOW I TURN JUNK INTO FUN AND PROFIT *Sari*    3.00
_____HOW TO PLAY THE HARMONICA FOR FUN & PROFIT *Hal Leighton*    3.00
_____HOW TO WRITE A HIT SONG & SELL IT *Tommy Boyce*    7.00
_____JUGGLING MADE EASY *Rudolf Dittrich*    2.00
_____MAGIC MADE EASY *Byron Wels*    2.00
_____STAMP COLLECTING FOR BEGINNERS *Burton Hobson*    2.00

## HORSE PLAYERS' WINNING GUIDES

_____BETTING HORSES TO WIN *Les Conklin*    3.00
_____ELIMINATE THE LOSERS *Bob McKnight*    3.00
_____HOW TO PICK WINNING HORSES *Bob McKnight*    3.00
_____HOW TO WIN AT THE RACES *Sam (The Genius) Lewin*    3.00
_____HOW YOU CAN BEAT THE RACES *Jack Kavanagh*    3.00

_____ MAKING MONEY AT THE RACES *David Barr* 3.00
_____ PAYDAY AT THE RACES *Les Conklin* 3.00
_____ SMART HANDICAPPING MADE EASY *William Bauman* 3.00
_____ SUCCESS AT THE HARNESS RACES *Barry Meadow* 3.00
_____ WINNING AT THE HARNESS RACES—An Expert's Guide *Nick Cammarano* 3.00

## HUMOR
_____ HOW TO BE A COMEDIAN FOR FUN & PROFIT *King & Laufer* 2.00
_____ HOW TO FLATTEN YOUR TUSH *Coach Marge Reardon* 2.00
_____ JOKE TELLER'S HANDBOOK *Bob Orben* 3.00
_____ JOKES FOR ALL OCCASIONS *Al Schock* 3.00
_____ 2000 NEW LAUGHS FOR SPEAKERS *Bob Orben* 3.00
_____ 2,500 JOKES TO START 'EM LAUGHING *Bob Orben* 3.00

## HYPNOTISM
_____ ADVANCED TECHNIQUES OF HYPNOSIS *Melvin Powers* 2.00
_____ BRAINWASHING AND THE CULTS *Paul A. Verdier, Ph.D.* 3.00
_____ CHILDBIRTH WITH HYPNOSIS *William S. Kroger, M.D.* 3.00
_____ HOW TO SOLVE Your Sex Problems with Self-Hypnosis *Frank S. Caprio, M.D.* 3.00
_____ HOW TO STOP SMOKING THRU SELF-HYPNOSIS *Leslie M. LeCron* 3.00
_____ HOW TO USE AUTO-SUGGESTION EFFECTIVELY *John Duckworth* 3.00
_____ HOW YOU CAN BOWL BETTER USING SELF-HYPNOSIS *Jack Heise* 3.00
_____ HOW YOU CAN PLAY BETTER GOLF USING SELF-HYPNOSIS *Jack Heise* 3.00
_____ HYPNOSIS AND SELF-HYPNOSIS *Bernard Hollander, M.D.* 3.00
_____ HYPNOTISM *(Originally published in 1893) Carl Sextus* 5.00
_____ HYPNOTISM & PSYCHIC PHENOMENA *Simeon Edmunds* 3.00
_____ HYPNOTISM MADE EASY *Dr. Ralph Winn* 3.00
_____ HYPNOTISM MADE PRACTICAL *Louis Orton* 3.00
_____ HYPNOTISM REVEALED *Melvin Powers* 2.00
_____ HYPNOTISM TODAY *Leslie LeCron and Jean Bordeaux, Ph.D.* 4.00
_____ MODERN HYPNOSIS *Lesley Kuhn & Salvatore Russo, Ph.D.* 5.00
_____ NEW CONCEPTS OF HYPNOSIS *Bernard C. Gindes, M.D.* 5.00
_____ NEW SELF-HYPNOSIS *Paul Adams* 4.00
_____ POST-HYPNOTIC INSTRUCTIONS—Suggestions for Therapy *Arnold Furst* 3.00
_____ PRACTICAL GUIDE TO SELF-HYPNOSIS *Melvin Powers* 3.00
_____ PRACTICAL HYPNOTISM *Philip Magonet, M.D.* 3.00
_____ SECRETS OF HYPNOTISM *S. J. Van Pelt, M.D.* 3.00
_____ SELF-HYPNOSIS A Conditioned-Response Technique *Laurance Sparks* 5.00
_____ SELF-HYPNOSIS Its Theory, Technique & Application *Melvin Powers* 3.00
_____ THERAPY THROUGH HYPNOSIS *edited by Raphael H. Rhodes* 4.00

## JUDAICA
_____ HOW TO LIVE A RICHER & FULLER LIFE *Rabbi Edgar F. Magnin* 2.00
_____ MODERN ISRAEL *Lily Edelman* 2.00
_____ ROMANCE OF HASSIDISM *Jacob S. Minkin* 2.50
_____ SERVICE OF THE HEART *Evelyn Garfiel, Ph.D.* 4.00
_____ STORY OF ISRAEL IN COINS *Jean & Maurice Gould* 2.00
_____ STORY OF ISRAEL IN STAMPS *Maxim & Gabriel Shamir* 1.00

## JUST FOR WOMEN
_____ COSMOPOLITAN'S GUIDE TO MARVELOUS MEN Fwd. by *Helen Gurley Brown* 3.00
_____ COSMOPOLITAN'S HANG-UP HANDBOOK Foreword by *Helen Gurley Brown* 4.00
_____ COSMOPOLITAN'S LOVE BOOK—A Guide to Ecstasy in Bed 4.00
_____ COSMOPOLITAN'S NEW ETIQUETTE GUIDE Fwd. by *Helen Gurley Brown* 4.00
_____ I AM A COMPLEAT WOMAN *Doris Hagopian & Karen O'Connor Sweeney* 3.00
_____ JUST FOR WOMEN—A Guide to the Female Body *Richard E. Sand, M.D.* 4.00
_____ NEW APPROACHES TO SEX IN MARRIAGE *John E. Eichenlaub, M.D.* 3.00
_____ SEXUALLY ADEQUATE FEMALE *Frank S. Caprio, M.D.* 3.00
_____ YOUR FIRST YEAR OF MARRIAGE *Dr. Tom McGinnis* 3.00

## MARRIAGE, SEX & PARENTHOOD
_____ ABILITY TO LOVE *Dr. Allan Fromme* 5.00
_____ ENCYCLOPEDIA OF MODERN SEX & LOVE TECHNIQUES *Macandrew* 4.00
_____ GUIDE TO SUCCESSFUL MARRIAGE *Drs. Albert Ellis & Robert Harper* 4.00
_____ HOW TO RAISE AN EMOTIONALLY HEALTHY, HAPPY CHILD *A. Ellis* 3.00
_____ IMPOTENCE & FRIGIDITY *Edwin W. Hirsch, M.D.* 3.00
_____ SEX WITHOUT GUILT *Albert Ellis, Ph.D.* 3.00
_____ SEXUALLY ADEQUATE MALE *Frank S. Caprio, M.D.* 3.00

## MELVIN POWERS' MAIL ORDER LIBRARY

| | |
|---|---|
| _____HOW TO GET RICH IN MAIL ORDER *Melvin Powers* | 10.00 |
| _____HOW TO WRITE A GOOD ADVERTISEMENT *Victor O. Schwab* | 15.00 |
| _____WORLD WIDE MAIL ORDER SHOPPER'S GUIDE *Eugene V. Moller* | 5.00 |

## METAPHYSICS & OCCULT

| | |
|---|---|
| _____BOOK OF TALISMANS, AMULETS & ZODIACAL GEMS *William Pavitt* | 4.00 |
| _____CONCENTRATION—A Guide to Mental Mastery *Mouni Sadhu* | **3.00** |
| _____CRITIQUES OF GOD *Edited by Peter Angeles* | 7.00 |
| _____DREAMS & OMENS REVEALED *Fred Gettings* | 3.00 |
| _____EXTRA-TERRESTRIAL INTELLIGENCE—The First Encounter | 6.00 |
| _____FORTUNE TELLING WITH CARDS *P. Foli* | 3.00 |
| _____HANDWRITING ANALYSIS MADE EASY *John Marley* | 3.00 |
| _____HANDWRITING TELLS *Nadya Olyanova* | 5.00 |
| _____HOW TO UNDERSTAND YOUR DREAMS *Geoffrey A. Dudley* | 3.00 |
| _____ILLUSTRATED YOGA *William Zorn* | 3.00 |
| _____IN DAYS OF GREAT PEACE *Mouni Sadhu* | 3.00 |
| _____KING SOLOMON'S TEMPLE IN THE MASONIC TRADITION *Alex Horne* | 5.00 |
| _____LSD—THE AGE OF MIND *Bernard Roseman* | 2.00 |
| _____MAGICIAN—His training and work *W. E. Butler* | 3.00 |
| _____MEDITATION *Mouni Sadhu* | 5.00 |
| _____MODERN NUMEROLOGY *Morris C. Goodman* | 3.00 |
| _____NUMEROLOGY—ITS FACTS AND SECRETS *Ariel Yvon Taylor* | 3.00 |
| _____NUMEROLOGY MADE EASY *W. Mykian* | 3.00 |
| _____PALMISTRY MADE EASY *Fred Gettings* | 3.00 |
| _____PALMISTRY MADE PRACTICAL *Elizabeth Daniels Squire* | 3.00 |
| _____PALMISTRY SECRETS REVEALED *Henry Frith* | 3.00 |
| _____PRACTICAL YOGA *Ernest Wood* | 3.00 |
| _____PROPHECY IN OUR TIME *Martin Ebon* | 2.50 |
| _____PSYCHOLOGY OF HANDWRITING *Nadya Olyanova* | 3.00 |
| _____SUPERSTITION—Are you superstitious? *Eric Maple* | 2.00 |
| _____TAROT *Mouni Sadhu* | 6.00 |
| _____TAROT OF THE BOHEMIANS *Papus* | 5.00 |
| _____WAYS TO SELF-REALIZATION *Mouni Sadhu* | 3.00 |
| _____WHAT YOUR HANDWRITING REVEALS *Albert E. Hughes* | 2.00 |
| _____WITCHCRAFT, MAGIC & OCCULTISM—A Fascinating History *W. B. Crow* | 5.00 |
| _____WITCHCRAFT—THE SIXTH SENSE *Justine Glass* | 3.00 |
| _____WORLD OF PSYCHIC RESEARCH *Hereward Carrington* | 2.00 |

## SELF-HELP & INSPIRATIONAL

| | |
|---|---|
| _____CYBERNETICS WITHIN US *Y. Saparina* | 3.00 |
| _____DAILY POWER FOR JOYFUL LIVING *Dr. Donald Curtis* | 3.00 |
| _____DYNAMIC THINKING *Melvin Powers* | 2.00 |
| _____EXUBERANCE—Your Guide to Happiness & Fulfillment *Dr. Paul Kurtz* | 3.00 |
| _____GREATEST POWER IN THE UNIVERSE *U. S. Andersen* | 4.00 |
| _____GROW RICH WHILE YOU SLEEP *Ben Sweetland* | 3.00 |
| _____GROWTH THROUGH REASON *Albert Ellis, Ph.D.* | 4.00 |
| _____GUIDE TO DEVELOPING YOUR POTENTIAL *Herbert A. Otto, Ph.D.* | 3.00 |
| _____GUIDE TO LIVING IN BALANCE *Frank S. Caprio, M.D.* | 2.00 |
| _____HELPING YOURSELF WITH APPLIED PSYCHOLOGY *R. Henderson* | 2.00 |
| _____HELPING YOURSELF WITH PSYCHIATRY *Frank S. Caprio, M.D.* | 2.00 |
| _____HOW TO ATTRACT GOOD LUCK *A. H. Z. Carr* | 3.00 |
| _____HOW TO CONTROL YOUR DESTINY *Norvell* | 3.00 |
| _____HOW TO DEVELOP A WINNING PERSONALITY *Martin Panzer* | 3.00 |
| _____HOW TO DEVELOP AN EXCEPTIONAL MEMORY *Young & Gibson* | 4.00 |
| _____HOW TO OVERCOME YOUR FEARS *M. P. Leahy, M.D.* | 3.00 |
| _____HOW YOU CAN HAVE CONFIDENCE AND POWER *Les Giblin* | 3.00 |
| _____HUMAN PROBLEMS & HOW TO SOLVE THEM *Dr. Donald Curtis* | 3.00 |
| _____I CAN *Ben Sweetland* | 4.00 |
| _____I WILL *Ben Sweetland* | 3.00 |
| _____LEFT-HANDED PEOPLE *Michael Barsley* | 4.00 |
| _____MAGIC IN YOUR MIND *U. S. Andersen* | 4.00 |
| _____MAGIC OF THINKING BIG *Dr. David J. Schwartz* | 3.00 |
| _____MAGIC POWER OF YOUR MIND *Walter M. Germain* | 4.00 |

_____ MENTAL POWER THROUGH SLEEP SUGGESTION *Melvin Powers* 3.00
_____ NEW GUIDE TO RATIONAL LIVING *Albert Ellis, Ph.D. & R. Harper, Ph.D.* 3.00
_____ OUR TROUBLED SELVES *Dr. Allan Fromme* 3.00
_____ PSYCHO-CYBERNETICS *Maxwell Maltz, M.D.* 2.00
_____ SCIENCE OF MIND IN DAILY LIVING *Dr. Donald Curtis* 3.00
_____ SECRET OF SECRETS *U. S. Andersen* 4.00
_____ SECRET POWER OF THE PYRAMIDS *U. S. Andersen* 4.00
_____ STUTTERING AND WHAT YOU CAN DO ABOUT IT *W. Johnson, Ph.D.* 2.50
_____ SUCCESS-CYBERNETICS *U. S. Andersen* 4.00
_____ 10 DAYS TO A GREAT NEW LIFE *William E. Edwards* 3.00
_____ THINK AND GROW RICH *Napoleon Hill* 3.00
_____ THREE MAGIC WORDS *U. S. Andersen* 5.00
_____ TREASURY OF COMFORT *edited by Rabbi Sidney Greenberg* 5.00
_____ TREASURY OF THE ART OF LIVING *Sidney S. Greenberg* 5.00
_____ YOU ARE NOT THE TARGET *Laura Huxley* 4.00
_____ YOUR SUBCONSCIOUS POWER *Charles M. Simmons* 4.00
_____ YOUR THOUGHTS CAN CHANGE YOUR LIFE *Dr. Donald Curtis* 3.00

### SPORTS

_____ ARCHERY—An Expert's Guide *Dan Stamp* 2.00
_____ BICYCLING FOR FUN AND GOOD HEALTH *Kenneth E. Luther* 2.00
_____ BILLIARDS—Pocket • Carom • Three Cushion *Clive Cottingham, Jr.* 3.00
_____ CAMPING-OUT 101 Ideas & Activities *Bruno Knobel* 2.00
_____ COMPLETE GUIDE TO FISHING *Vlad Evanoff* 2.00
_____ HOW TO IMPROVE YOUR RACQUETBALL *Lubarsky, Kaufman, & Scagnetti* 3.00
_____ HOW TO WIN AT POCKET BILLIARDS *Edward D. Knuchell* 4.00
_____ JOY OF WALKING *Jack Scagnetti* 3.00
_____ LEARNING & TEACHING SOCCER SKILLS *Eric Worthington* 3.00
_____ MOTORCYCLING FOR BEGINNERS *I. G. Edmonds* 3.00
_____ RACQUETBALL FOR WOMEN *Toni Hudson, Jack Scagnetti & Vince Rondone* 3.00
_____ RACQUETBALL MADE EASY *Steve Lubarsky, Rod Delson & Jack Scagnetti* 3.00
_____ SECRET OF BOWLING STRIKES *Dawson Taylor* 3.00
_____ SECRET OF PERFECT PUTTING *Horton Smith & Dawson Taylor* 3.00
_____ SOCCER—The game & how to play it *Gary Rosenthal* 3.00
_____ STARTING SOCCER *Edward F. Dolan, Jr.* 3.00
_____ TABLE TENNIS MADE EASY *Johnny Leach* 2.00

### TENNIS LOVERS' LIBRARY

_____ BEGINNER'S GUIDE TO WINNING TENNIS *Helen Hull Jacobs* 2.00
_____ HOW TO BEAT BETTER TENNIS PLAYERS *Loring Fiske* 4.00
_____ HOW TO IMPROVE YOUR TENNIS—Style, Strategy & Analysis *C. Wilson* 2.00
_____ INSIDE TENNIS—Techniques of Winning *Jim Leighton* 3.00
_____ PLAY TENNIS WITH ROSEWALL *Ken Rosewall* 2.00
_____ PSYCH YOURSELF TO BETTER TENNIS *Dr. Walter A. Luszki* 2.00
_____ SUCCESSFUL TENNIS *Neale Fraser* 2.00
_____ TENNIS FOR BEGINNERS *Dr. H. A. Murray* 2.00
_____ TENNIS MADE EASY *Joel Brecheen* 2.00
_____ WEEKEND TENNIS—How to have fun & win at the same time *Bill Talbert* 3.00
_____ WINNING WITH PERCENTAGE TENNIS—Smart Strategy *Jack Lowe* 2.00

### WILSHIRE PET LIBRARY

_____ DOG OBEDIENCE TRAINING *Gust Kessopulos* 4.00
_____ DOG TRAINING MADE EASY & FUN *John W. Kellogg* 3.00
_____ HOW TO BRING UP YOUR PET DOG *Kurt Unkelbach* 2.00
_____ HOW TO RAISE & TRAIN YOUR PUPPY *Jeff Griffen* 2.00
_____ PIGEONS: HOW TO RAISE & TRAIN THEM *William H. Allen, Jr.* 2.00

*The books listed above can be obtained from your book dealer or directly from*
*Melvin Powers. When ordering, please remit 50¢ per book postage & handling.*
*Send for our free illustrated catalog of self-improvement books.*

## Melvin Powers
12015 Sherman Road, No. Hollywood, California 91605

## WILSHIRE HORSE LOVERS' LIBRARY

| | |
|---|---:|
| _____ AMATEUR HORSE BREEDER *A. C. Leighton Hardman* | 3.00 |
| _____ AMERICAN QUARTER HORSE IN PICTURES *Margaret Cabell Self* | 3.00 |
| _____ APPALOOSA HORSE *Donna & Bill Richardson* | 3.00 |
| _____ ARABIAN HORSE *Reginald S. Summerhays* | 2.00 |
| _____ ART OF WESTERN RIDING *Suzanne Norton Jones* | 3.00 |
| _____ AT THE HORSE SHOW *Margaret Cabell Self* | 3.00 |
| _____ BACK-YARD FOAL *Peggy Jett Pittinger* | 3.00 |
| _____ BACK-YARD HORSE *Peggy Jett Pittinger* | 3.00 |
| _____ BASIC DRESSAGE *Jean Froissard* | 2.00 |
| _____ BEGINNER'S GUIDE TO HORSEBACK RIDING *Sheila Wall* | 2.00 |
| _____ BEGINNER'S GUIDE TO THE WESTERN HORSE *Natlee Kenoyer* | 2.00 |
| _____ BITS—THEIR HISTORY, USE AND MISUSE *Louis Taylor* | 3.00 |
| _____ BREAKING & TRAINING THE DRIVING HORSE *Doris Ganton* | 3.00 |
| _____ BREAKING YOUR HORSE'S BAD HABITS *W. Dayton Sumner* | 3.00 |
| _____ CAVALRY MANUAL OF HORSEMANSHIP *Gordon Wright* | 3.00 |
| _____ COMPLETE TRAINING OF HORSE AND RIDER *Colonel Alois Podhajsky* | 4.00 |
| _____ DISORDERS OF THE HORSE & WHAT TO DO ABOUT THEM *E. Hanauer* | 3.00 |
| _____ DOG TRAINING MADE EASY & FUN *John W. Kellogg* | 3.00 |
| _____ DRESSAGE—A Study of the Finer Points in Riding *Henry Wynmalen* | 4.00 |
| _____ DRIVING HORSES *Sallie Walrond* | 3.00 |
| _____ ENDURANCE RIDING *Ann Hyland* | 2.00 |
| _____ EQUITATION *Jean Froissard* | 4.00 |
| _____ FIRST AID FOR HORSES *Dr. Charles H. Denning, Jr.* | 2.00 |
| _____ FUN OF RAISING A COLT *Rubye & Frank Griffith* | 3.00 |
| _____ FUN ON HORSEBACK *Margaret Cabell Self* | 4.00 |
| _____ GYMKHANA GAMES *Natlee Kenoyer* | 2.00 |
| _____ HORSE DISEASES—Causes, Symptoms & Treatment *Dr. H. G. Belschner* | 4.00 |
| _____ HORSE OWNER'S CONCISE GUIDE *Elsie V. Hanauer* | 2.00 |
| _____ HORSE SELECTION & CARE FOR BEGINNERS *George H. Conn* | 4.00 |
| _____ HORSE SENSE—A complete guide to riding and care *Alan Deacon* | 4.00 |
| _____ HORSEBACK RIDING FOR BEGINNERS *Louis Taylor* | 4.00 |
| _____ HORSEBACK RIDING MADE EASY & FUN *Sue Henderson Coen* | 4.00 |
| _____ HORSES—Their Selection, Care & Handling *Margaret Cabell Self* | 3.00 |
| _____ HOW TO BUY A BETTER HORSE & SELL THE HORSE YOU OWN | 3.00 |
| _____ HOW TO ENJOY YOUR QUARTER HORSE *Williard H. Porter* | 3.00 |
| _____ HUNTER IN PICTURES *Margaret Cabell Self* | 2.00 |
| _____ ILLUSTRATED BOOK OF THE HORSE *S. Sidney* (8½″ x 11″) | 10.00 |
| _____ ILLUSTRATED HORSE MANAGEMENT—400 Illustrations *Dr. E. Mayhew* | 6.00 |
| _____ ILLUSTRATED HORSE TRAINING *Captain M. H. Hayes* | 5.00 |
| _____ ILLUSTRATED HORSEBACK RIDING FOR BEGINNERS *Jeanne Mellin* | 2.00 |
| _____ JUMPING—Learning & Teaching *Jean Froissard* | 4.00 |
| _____ KNOW ALL ABOUT HORSES *Harry Disston* | 3.00 |
| _____ LAME HORSE—Causes, Symptoms & Treatment *Dr. James R. Rooney* | 4.00 |
| _____ LAW & YOUR HORSE *Edward H. Greene* | 5.00 |
| _____ LIPIZZANERS & THE SPANISH RIDING SCHOOL *W. Reuter* (4¼″ x 6″) | 2.50 |
| _____ MANUAL OF HORSEMANSHIP *Harold Black* | 5.00 |
| _____ MORGAN HORSE IN PICTURES *Margaret Cabell Self* | 2.00 |
| _____ MOVIE HORSES—The Fascinating Techniques of Training *Anthony Amaral* | 2.00 |
| _____ POLICE HORSES *Judith Campbell* | 2.00 |
| _____ PRACTICAL GUIDE TO HORSESHOEING | 3.00 |
| _____ PRACTICAL GUIDE TO OWNING YOUR OWN HORSE *Steven D. Price* | 2.00 |
| _____ PRACTICAL HORSE PSYCHOLOGY *Moyra Williams* | 3.00 |
| _____ PROBLEM HORSES Guide for Curing Serious Behavior Habits *Summerhays* | 3.00 |
| _____ REINSMAN OF THE WEST—BRIDLES & BITS *Ed Connell* | 4.00 |
| _____ RESCHOOLING THE THOROUGHBRED *Peggy Jett Pittenger* | 3.00 |
| _____ RIDE WESTERN *Louis Taylor* | 3.00 |
| _____ SCHOOLING YOUR YOUNG HORSE *George Wheatley* | 2.00 |
| _____ STABLE MANAGEMENT FOR THE OWNER-GROOM *George Wheatley* | 4.00 |
| _____ STALLION MANAGEMENT—A Guide for Stud Owners *A. C. Hardman* | 3.00 |
| _____ TEACHING YOUR HORSE TO JUMP *W. J. Froud* | 2.00 |
| _____ TRAIL HORSES & TRAIL RIDING *Anne & Perry Westbrook* | 2.00 |
| _____ TRAINING YOUR HORSE TO SHOW *Neale Haley* | 4.00 |
| _____ TREATING COMMON DISEASES OF YOUR HORSE *Dr. George H. Conn* | 3.00 |
| _____ TREATING HORSE AILMENTS *G. W. Serth* | 2.00 |
| _____ WESTERN HORSEBACK RIDING *Glen Balch* | 3.00 |
| _____ YOU AND YOUR PONY *Pepper Mainwaring Healey* (8½″ x 11″) | 6.00 |
| _____ YOUR FIRST HORSE *George C. Saunders, M.D.* | 3.00 |
| _____ YOUR PONY BOOK *Hermann Wiederhold* | 2.00 |
| _____ YOUR WESTERN HORSE *Nelson C. Nye* | 2.00 |

*The books listed above can be obtained from your book dealer or directly from
Melvin Powers. When ordering, please remit 50¢ per book postage & handling.
Send for our free illustrated catalog of self-improvement books.*

## Melvin Powers
12015 Sherman Road, No. Hollywood, California 91605

## *Melvin Powers' Favorite Books*

# HOW TO GET RICH IN MAIL ORDER
### *by Melvin Powers*
Contents:
1. How to Develop Your Mail Order Expertise 2. How to Find a Unique Product or Service to Sell 3. How to Make Money with Classified Ads 4. How to Make Money with Display Ads 5. The Unlimited Potential for Making Money with Direct Mail 6. How to Copycat Successful Mail Order Operations 7. How I Created A Best Seller Using the Copycat Technique 8. How to Start and Run a Profitable Mail Order, Special Interest Book or Record Business 9. I Enjoy Selling Books by Mail—Some of My Successful and Not-So-Successful Ads and Direct Mail Circulars 10. Five of My Most Successful Direct Mail Pieces That Sold and Are Still Selling Millions of Dollars Worth of Books 11. Melvin Powers' Mail Order Success Strategy—Follow It and You'll Become a Millionaire 12. How to Sell Your Products to Mail Order Companies, Retail Outlets, Jobbers, and Fund Raisers for Maximum Distribution and Profits 13. How to Get Free Display Ads and Publicity That Can Put You on the Road to Riches 14. How to Make Your Advertising Copy Sizzle to Make You Wealthy 15. Questions and Answers to Help You Get Started Making Money in Your Own Mail Order Business 16. A Personal Word from Melvin Powers

8½"x 11"—336 Pages . . . $11 postpaid

# HOW YOU CAN HAVE CONFIDENCE & POWER
### *by Les Giblin*
Contents:
1. Your Key to Success and Happiness 2. How to Use the Basic Secret for Influencing Others 3. How to Cash in on Your Hidden Assets 4. How to Control the Actions & Attitudes of Others 5. How You Can Create a Good Impression on Other People 6. Techniques for Making & Keeping Friends 7. How to Use Three Big Secrets for Attracting People 8. How to Make the Other Person Feel Friendly—Instantly

192 Pages . . . $3.50 postpaid

# A NEW GUIDE TO RATIONAL LIVING
### *by Albert Ellis, Ph.D. & Robert A. Harper, Ph.D.*
Contents:
1. How Far Can You Go With Self-Analysis? 2. You Feel the Way You Think 3. Feeling Well by Thinking Straight 4. How You Create Your Feelings 5. Thinking Yourself Out of Emotional Disturbances 6. Recognizing and Attacking Neurotic Behavior 7. Overcoming the Influences of the Past 8. Does Reason Always Prove Reasonable? 9. Refusing to Feel Desperately Unhappy 10. Tackling Dire Needs for Approval 11. Eradicating Dire Fears of Failure 12. How to Stop Blaming and Start Living 13. How to Feel Undepressed though Frustrated 14. Controlling Your Own Destiny 15. Conquering Anxiety

256 Pages . . . $3.50 postpaid

# PSYCHO-CYBERNETICS
A New Technique for Using Your Subconscious Power
### *by Maxwell Maltz, M.D., F.I.C.S.*
Contents:
1. The Self Image: Your Key to a Better Life 2. Discovering the Success Mechanism Within You 3. Imagination—The First Key to Your Success Mechanism 4. Dehypnotize Yourself from False Beliefs 5. How to Utilize the Power of Rational Thinking 6. Relax and Let Your Success Mechanism Work for You 7. You Can Acquire the Habit of Happiness 8. Ingredients of the Success-Type Personality and How to Acquire Them 9. The Failure Mechanism: How to Make It Work For You Instead of Against You 10. How to Remove Emotional Scars, or How to Give Yourself an Emotional Face Lift 11. How to Unlock Your Real Personality 12. Do-It-Yourself Tranquilizers

288 Pages . . . $2.50 postpaid

# A PRACTICAL GUIDE TO SELF-HYPNOSIS
### *by Melvin Powers*
Contents:
1. What You Should Know About Self-Hypnosis 2. What About the Dangers of Hypnosis? 3. Is Hypnosis the Answer? 4. How Does Self-Hypnosis Work? 5. How to Arouse Yourself from the Self-Hypnotic State 6. How to Attain Self-Hypnosis 7. Deepening the Self-Hypnotic State 8. What You Should Know About Becoming an Excellent Subject 9. Techniques for Reaching the Somnambulistic State 10. A New Approach to Self-Hypnosis When All Else Fails 11. Psychological Aids and Their Function 12. The Nature of Hypnosis 13. Practical Applications of Self-Hypnosis.

128 Pages . . . $3.50 postpaid

*The books listed above can be obtained from your book dealer or directly from Melvin Powers.*

# Melvin Powers
12015 Sherman Road, No. Hollywood, California 91605